Susan Heerema

Debbie

Sept. 2, 1992

Dear Doug,

    Thanks for all of your help,
guidance, and friendship.
We will all miss you.

      Care Choices Staff

Cindy Neville

Dorothea

Nancy Buchman

Maryann Mills

Jan Brandt

Patty Sanford

Melissa Lambers

Linda VanderPloeg

Kathy Engel

Michelle Marvin

Wood, Water & Light

Wood, Water & Light
CLASSIC WOODEN BOATS

Text by Joel White

Photographs by Benjamin Mendlowitz

W. W. NORTON & COMPANY
NEW YORK · LONDON

This book is dedicated to Anne and Maynard Bray,
together with all other guardians of fine wooden
boats whose love, care, and hard work assures
the survival of these beautiful craft.

Photographs Copyright © 1988 by Benjamin Mendlowitz
Text Copyright © 1988 by Joel White
All rights reserved.

Library of Congress Cataloging in Publication Data
Mendlowitz, Benjamin
Wood, Water & Light / Benjamin Mendlowitz and Joel White
p. cm.
1. Boats and boating—Pictorial works. I. White, Joel.
II. Title. III. Wood Water & Light.
VM321.M46 1988
387.2'23'0222—dc19   88–5870

The text of this book was composed in Monotype Dante
by Michael & Winifred Bixler
Printed and bound in Italy by Arnoldo Mondadori Editore, Verona
Book design by Sherry Streeter

ISBN 0-393-03327-9

W.W. Norton & Company, Inc., 500 Fifth Avenue, New York, N.Y. 10110
W.W. Norton & Company Ltd., 10 Coptic Street, London WC1A 1PU

2 3 4 5 6 7 8 9 10

Contents

Foreword

WOOD, WATER, AND LIGHT: the words alone seem to evoke elemental images of beauty and magic, and in their blending we sense a wonderful alchemy. It is not so farfetched: each element has its own power to transform and transport us. The warmth of wood, the embrace of water, and the constant play of light. Small wonder, then, that a collection of words and images which celebrate these powerful elements can create so lovely a work as this.

There is an irresistible aura about boats and yachts built of wood, an aura brimming over with the richness of creation. It flows from the strength and grace of trees themselves, through the hands of craftsmen who fashion them into proud new forms. It is the presence not only of substance but of soul, created in a collaboration between the earth, the sea, and the artisans who fit the wood with skill and care so that it will look lovely and last long. It is these qualities, so hard to describe yet so easily felt, which distinguish our appreciation for fine wooden boats and yachts. They are not merely waterborne conveyances; they are not simply floating palaces large and small: they are expressions of an ancient art evolved over centuries of time and tide. And they appear in a vast array of graceful forms. This book is both a celebration and an appreciation of these.

Giving voice to this appreciation is not a simple matter. It requires a photographer with a passion for these boats and a keen eye for light and shadow. It requires a writer with the same passion combined with a deep understanding of form and function and structure, and of how they work together. Benjamin Mendlowitz and Joel White meet these criteria and more, and they have joined to produce a hymn to the present and future of wooden boats. They have done so with a unique sense of care and commitment, and they have found in their publisher a willing partner. It would be easy to produce a book of fine photographs, with a few captions to tie them all together. But the authors seek more than this, and the publisher has seen fit to provide fine bookmaking.

Within these pages are images and essays on some two dozen boats and yachts. Accompanying each boat is a lovely profile drawing revealing the underwater character of the craft, and an arrangement rendering of the interior layouts or structures. The result of this considerable effort is a gratifyingly complete picture of the various boats and yachts featured. And the subjects themselves are most wonderful examples of the art and science of wooden boat building. From the dainty sailing canoe *Twilite* to the rugged schooner *Heritage* and the aircraft-engine-powered, 70-knot cruiser *Thunderbird*, the wooden boats celebrated herein represent some of the finest ever designed and built.

There are classic cruising yachts, both sail and power, built to transport their owners in a style reflecting their nature. From the functional simplicity and unusual grace of the little yawl *Annie* to the subtle, old-world elegance of the power yacht *Canim*, with her carved moldings and marble fireplace, or *Aida*, lovingly cared for, skillfully sailed, a full-fledged member of her family. There are classic racers, like the vintage 12-meter *Gleam*, the 50-foot P-class sloop *Chips*, the still-active fleet of Dark Harbor 20s, and the extraordinary Gold Cup racer *Baby Bootlegger*. Such craft leave us breathless in their passing. There are the charming smaller craft, which include such wonders as the Herreshoff 12½s, one of the most beautiful small boat classes ever created, and the Beetle Cats, the oldest wooden one-designs in continuous production today. Both of these classes have taught generations of youngsters how to play well with wind and wave. The traditional Maine peapods, which served the inshore fishermen so well and so long, were among the most versatile and functional open boats ever devised. They have become pleasure boats now, well suited to their new callings. And there are the classic working boats: the sardine carriers, required to be eminently seaworthy and swift whether their holds were empty or full; the *Unity B*, designed, built, and worked under sail by her owner, who carries her cargo to market at Nassau, and sells it himself at the quayside; and the lobsterboats, some of the last of a vanishing breed of boat, once designed and built in great but subtle variety along the New England coast.

In evidence here is the breadth and diversity of the wooden boat tradition, the commitment of designers, builders, and owners to a level of craftsmanship and excellence too rarely seen any more. It is a sign of hope for the future that there are still individuals who care about preserving such craft as these in the world. The nature of the things we care about has changed, as it always must, but we should endeavor to remember that anything built by hand and eye, with love and care, deserves our deepest appreciation.

The words and images which follow are simple and unpretentious ones, expressing nothing less than a deep caring for quality, integrity, and graceful elegance. Yet in their very capturing of the richness of these elements, they are profoundly inspiring. This is a book to be savored again and again, to be returned to for sustenance in those times when there is little evidence of grace and beauty on the water. It is a celebration of the past and the present, to be sure. But it is also a celebration of the future, for we have not yet lost our ability to understand and appreciate the uniqueness of the wooden boat.

Jonathan Wilson, Editor
WoodenBoat Magazine

Author's Introduction

A BOOK OF PHOTOGRAPHS is not perceived by the reader in the same way as a book of words. Visual perception of a photographic image is nearly instantaneous; the printed word requires a finite time-lag. For this reason a photograph, or better yet, a collection of them, can have dramatic impact not possible with text alone. I think you will agree this collection has impact.

Benjamin Mendlowitz, a near neighbor of mine, is perhaps America's best photographer of wooden boats, and between these covers are some of his finest pictures of a number of these boats. What you see here is a sampling of the handsomest, best cared-for, and most interesting wooden boats in the world. The criteria for inclusion in this book are simple: the boat must be photogenic, must be wooden, and must be a good boat. The first and last of these criteria are purely subjective, and Benjamin and I have allowed our own preferences to have full sway. Fortunately, our tastes coincide very well, and we have had no problems between ourselves in choosing candidates.

Some of the boats included are old friends; several are moored in the harbor just outside my office window. Lobsterboats, peapods, sardine carriers, and coasting schooners are a part of the maritime scene in down-East Maine, where I live. Others are new to me. A great part of the pleasure of doing this book has been to discover, through these photographs, and my subsequent research, fine wooden boats from other parts of the world. In our selections, we have tried for diversity and contrast to stimulate the reader's interest, and hope we have succeeded. It is also comforting to discover, through the selection process, that we have just scratched the surface of the available candidates.

Sherry Streeter, a talented book and magazine designer, is responsible for the design of this volume. The visual pleasure which it brings to you is her doing. She was instrumental in developing the concept, selecting the photographs, and of course did all the layout work. Her touch enhances the finished product, and most importantly, the drama of the pictures.

Kathy Bray drew the handsome profile and arrangement plans shown at the beginning and end of each chapter. We felt it would be helpful to the reader to present each boat in a graphic way, to offer a view of the shape and the layout that may not be clearly shown in the selected photographs. While we have tried to work from original plans and drawings for this art work, in some cases no drawings were available. For instance, *Unity B*, the Bahamian sloop, was built by her owner entirely without plans. The sardine carrier *Pauline* was built from a half model. There are no plans in existence for *Fleetwood II*, the Canadian runabout, or for *Jericho*. For *Canim*, we had to modify plans of a sister-ship for the profile and estimate the interior layout from photos and descriptions. The lobsterboat shown is not a particular boat, only a typical one. In each case, I have attempted to reconstruct as accurately as possible a plan from which Kathy could work. I apologize for whatever inaccuracies that may have crept in.

For all those who helped me in researching the backgrounds of these boats, my sincere thanks. In some cases, the owners of the boats were contacted and were most generous with time and information. My wife Allene was always ready with encouragement and good editing. Particular thanks go to Wooden-Boat Magazine for the use of drawings and their excellent research library, staffed by Anne Bray and Cynthia Curtis. And to Maynard Bray, always a goldmine of boating information.

On rereading these essays, I discovered running through many of them a thread of wistful lament for changing times. This was not intentional; nevertheless it is there. I have been around long enough to know that there is always change, and that the world of wooden boats is not immune from it. It is an incontrovertible fact that working wooden boats are becoming more scarce each year. The wooden lobsterboats, the sardine carriers, the *Unity B*'s are dwindling in number, and with few new ones being built, are yielding to boats built of newer materials—steel, aluminum, and fiberglass. The wooden boat, however, will not vanish in my lifetime, nor in yours; fine wooden boats are being built every day. If the photographs and the text in this book can convey some sense of what is unique about wooden boats—explaining the delight we feel when watching *Cirrus* sail by—then we have made a contribution toward preserving these boats, and perhaps helped to inspire the creation of new ones.

Joel White
Brooklin, Maine

Photographer's Introduction

THE PHOTOGRAPHS PRESENTED in this book are a result of ten years of work with boating magazines, as well as time spent creating images for the *Calendar of Wooden Boats* which Maynard Bray, Sherry Streeter and I have turned out each year since 1983. Although each photography session is a story in itself, there are some common techniques and technical information that may be of interest to the reader.

When photographing a boat in an anchorage or underway, I prefer to be in a chase boat that enables me to move to the best angle and distance for my favorite lenses, or to follow along waiting for the right moment of boat speed, wave movement and crew action. When working in Maine I often use my 20 foot outboard-powered lapstrake runabout, *Motordrive*. She's fairly dry, very maneuverable and able to handle most summer wave conditions in our protected waters. Although at times I struggle alone, driving and shooting, the best photographs seem to come when I work with Maynard Bray. He is not only a superb boat handler but has the all-important ability to set up shots instinctively, with little need for discussion that can waste the instant of the best shot.

Many of the best-known images from the early years of marine photography were made on large format negatives. However, the speed and ease of handling a 35mm camera, especially one that is motor driven, along with the luxury of 36 exposures per roll are irresistible to today's marine photographers. All the photographs in this book were shot on 35mm Kodachrome 64 film, using Nikon F and F3 cameras and lenses. My concerns for image quality and the longevity of the original slides have made me limit my film selection to Kodachrome. Although Kodachrome 25 has a slightly finer grain, the added speed offered by the ISO 64 emulsion allows me to continue to shoot as the light level goes down and use the higher shutter speeds needed for hand-held photography on the water.

I use fixed-focal-length Nikkor lenses, and although I carry a wide range from 20mm to 300mm most of my shots are made using a 50mm or 105mm lens. These lenses yield an accurate and pleasing rendition of the shapes of classic boats, whose beautiful sheers and lines should not, in my mind, be distorted by the use of either an extreme wide angle or telephoto lens. When shooting on deck or down below I will, however, often select a 35mm or 24mm lens to show a bit more sail and water along with the view on deck, or in an effort to include enough of the interior in a single shot. I try to take care when working with these lenses to keep the camera's film plane parallel to the vertical lines in the image. This technique limits the apparent distortion common with wide angle photography.

Although on rare occasion I will use a polarizing filter to darken the sky, the vast majority of my shots are made with unmanipulated natural light. At times I will light the interior of a shop or boat with flash or quartz lights. When possible I prefer to work with the available light—adjusting light and dark areas by opening or blocking off doors, windows, hatches, ports, etc. All but one or two of the photographs in this book, whether exterior or interior, were made with unfiltered available light.

These photographs and this book have been made possible by the generosity of many fine people encountered through my work. I would like especially to thank: the editors and art directors of *Nautical Quarterly, Sail* and *Wooden-Boat* magazines who have consistently published my pictures—without their support and assignments many of these photographs would never have been created; all the boat owners who have been kind enough to allow me to photograph their vessels—for their patience, when I shot during a race, and for their efforts in sprucing up and maneuvering for the benefit of my camera; Joel White for taking time from his yacht design work and busy Brooklin Boat Yard —which builds and maintains some of the finest wooden boats on the coast of Maine—to do a thorough and excellent job of research and writing for this book; Sherry Streeter for devoting her design talents to the project, and for her respect for the author's and photographer's concerns and opinions; Kathy Bray for her fine drawings of each boat; Jim Mairs, our editor at W.W. Norton, for his faith in this project and steadfast commitment to printing quality; my wife Deborah and son Will for help while shooting and with photo selection, as well as cheerfully enduring early morning, late night and weekend work.

Benjamin Mendlowitz
Brooklin, Maine

Wood, Water & Light

AIDA

is a lucky boat. Designed and built by Herreshoff of Bristol, she is owned by Anne and Maynard Bray, two of the most enthusiastic and capable Herreshoff buffs anywhere. It is obvious that *Aida*, treated as a member of the family, thrives on their love and care.

LOA: 33' 6"
LWL: 27' 0"
Beam: 9' 2"
Draft: 3' 0"

Each fall, *Aida* is taken from the waters of Eggemoggin Reach, carefully placed on her special trailer, and hauled over the road to her own boathouse behind the Bray residence. Winter projects are planned and executed, and in the spring the full force of the Bray fitting-out philosophy is brought to bear on her needs and problems. Anne is a master varnisher, and *Aida*'s brightwork bears witness to this. The aim of the program is protecting the surfaces and the boat, not producing a glossy finish. Flat and semi-gloss paints prevail, with old-fashioned soft copper paint being used on the bottom—not the flashiest, but stuff that works. When she slips back into her element in the early summer, she always looks great.

The Brays use her a lot. She is off her mooring more than she is on it. Week-long cruises, day sails, moonlit evening jaunts—*Aida* is going all the time. Respecting her years and the fact that her bottom is original and unrebuilt, the Brays sail her with care and restraint. They don't take her offshore, they don't drive her to windward in a gale. I can't believe that either the boat or the Brays have any less fun because of the restrictions.

She really is the perfect boat for Maynard and Anne. A slightly enlarged version of Nat Herreshoff's own boat *Pleasure*, she was built in 1926. Largely unchanged below, she is very simple but very elegant. White painted panelled bulkheads, four berths, a galley, an enclosed head—it would be hard to find an interior that makes less fuss, or more sense. Her cockpit is long and spacious, just right for a crowd on a sail or enjoying the sunset at anchor.

If one was to speculate on *Aida*'s pedigree, one would have to conclude that Captain Nat's own *Alerion*, built in 1912, was the beginning of the line. This lovely twenty-six foot sloop was used by Herreshoff in Bermuda where he

vacationed each winter. *Alerion* is now on permanent display at Mystic Seaport Museum, where she is one of the most prized and admired exhibits. *Aida* reminds me of *Alerion*, but half again as big and somewhat stouter. Both are centerboarders, and have similar profiles and sections. *Aida's* cabin is long, to give space for cruising accommodations, while *Alerion's* small cuddy had only to provide shelter for sails and a picnic basket. *Aida* is yawl rigged for easier sail handling, but she still seems to me like a robust version of *Alerion*.

Aida's rig had been reduced in size by a previous owner. Maynard, not content with ordinary standards of speed under sail, has lengthened her mast five feet to its original height, bought a complete suit of new sails, and installed a folding propeller. Now no one can catch her under most conditions, and she is winning local races with alarming regularity. Maynard has described her, in print, as "a wholesome little cruiser." Well, she is that, but she is mighty slippery to boot. No wonder Nat Herreshoff was called "wizard."

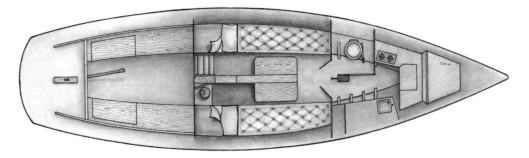

Designer: N. G. Herreshoff   Builder: Herreshoff Mfg. Co., 1926

INTERMEZZO

is a twelve foot wooden yacht dinghy. But not just any yacht dinghy—she is the epitome of what such a dinghy should be. Before the coming of fiberglass, great care and effort were sometimes lavished on these boats, as tiny representatives of their larger mother ship. In effect miniscule yachts themselves, some of the dinghies of generations past were lovely expressions of man's delight in subtle shapes and careful craftsmanship. *Intermezzo* is a fine example of small craft in this tradition.

LOA: 12' 3"
LWL: 11' 2"
Beam: 4' 6"
Draft: 0' 9"

The late Eddie Crosby was the designer of *Intermezzo*. After a circumnavigation while a young man, as mate of the schooner *Yankee* under Captain Irving Johnson, he returned to his native Cape Cod and became active in his father's boatyard, Chester A. Crosby and Sons. There he helped in managing the yard, as well as doing model-making, ships carving, and designing. *Intermezzo* was the last design before his untimely death.

Just because a boat is very small does not mean that its design is simple. A little dinghy such as this must accomplish several tasks: it must be able to carry heavy loads, to be easily rowed when both loaded and light, strong enough to withstand hard usage, yet light enough to be carried on deck or on davits of a larger yacht, and able to withstand drying out when carried clear of the water. The lapstrake construction used on *Intermezzo* is both strong and light, and resists drying out better than carvel planking.

Every piece, every surface of a little craft like this one is visible, is open for

inspection and scrutiny, unlike larger vessels where much of the structure is covered by ceiling, interior joinerwork, or is simply not exposed to view. Little boats such as this are often a showcase for some of the most exquisite boat-building skills and intricate constructional details to be seen anywhere. Eddie Crosby and the Crosby boatyard took advantage of this job to show off their knowledge and abilities. She is built with lapstrake cedar planking riveted to oak steam-bent frames, with mahogany garboards and sheer strakes. Seats and

stern are mahogany, floorboards teak, and her oars, made by Crosby himself, are spruce. Notice the continuous ash inwales which run from stern to stem and back to stern in one piece, and form comfortable lifting handles at the quarter knees. Two lathe-turned posts support the center thwarts. Special high-posted brass oarlocks keep the oars from chafing the gunwales and eliminate the need for gunwale blocks. Her sheer is highlighted by a rope gunwale guard, once the standard method of protecting a yacht's topsides from the depredations of its dinghy, but seldom seen nowadays. All in all, a classy piece of work, from design to gold-leafed name on the transom.

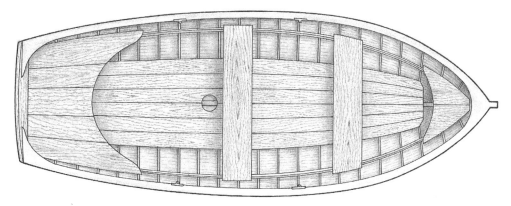

Designer: Edward Crosby   *Builder: Chester A. Crosby & Sons, 1979*

FLEETWOOD II —a nice word juxtaposition to describe
this swift runabout built of our favorite
boatbuilding material. This twenty-six foot mahogany launch was produced
during the winter of 1929 in Bracebridge, Ontario, on Lake Muskoka, by the
Minett-Shields Company, Ltd.

LOA: 26' 0"
LWL: 25' 3"
Beam: 6' 0"
Draft: 1' 0"

Lake Muskoka? I must confess that I had not heard of Lake Muskoka until
doing research on *Fleetwood II*. But it sounds to be a place where I must go some-
time: three connected lakes, Joseph, Rosseau, and Muskoka, deep in the woods
north of Toronto, provide the setting for an old-fashioned summer colony for
American and Canadian families that come year after year, generation after
generation, to refresh themselves at the lakes during the long summer days.
Handsome wooden cottages and boathouses dot the wooded shores and islands;
many of the boathouses shelter fine old wooden runabouts such as *Fleetwood* in
almost daily use around the lakes. Indeed this is a place that I must visit. I am a
salt-water dweller, but I admit that there is something that happens on a lake
deep in the woods—time flows more slowly there, and contentment seems to
rise from the surface of the water.

These Canadian lakes, it turns out, used to be a hotbed of wooden boatbuilding. There was, during the early years of the century, a brisk demand for
utility launches and faster runabouts to serve the needs of the families in summer residence along the lakefront. Over the years, a dozen or so boat companies
were formed. Some prospered until World War II, others did not and closed.

H. C. Minett Boatworks, which later became Minett-Shields Ltd., prospered better than most and remained in business until 1948.

An interesting book called "The Boatbuilders of Muskoka," by A. H. Duke and W. M. Gray, chronicles the banner days of Muskoka boatbuilding. H. C. (Bert) Minett, founder of Minett Boatworks, was considered by many on the lakes to be the finest craftsman of his time. A long series of lovely-looking runabouts, of both the displacement and later the planing type, attest to his skill. He not only was in charge of construction but designed most of the boats built by the company.

Through the courtesy of the present owner of *Fleetwood*, Mr. Gray, and his son, I have a copy of her original specifications prepared by Minett-Shields Ltd. —four pages of interesting reading.

> Stem: *our special design patented No. 12 aluminum with tamerac (sic.) back rabbet bent in one piece from head of stem to four feet aft on keel and bolted to stem and keel by brass bolts.*
>
> Delivery: *boat is to be delivered at the owner's residence May 24th, 1929 and in a complete and proper running order.*

There is considerable use made of local materials—Lake Erie white oak and Ontario cedar are both mentioned, but mahogany was specified for topside planking and decking. Upholstery was to be "real leather #1 quality pleated style." Much of the hardware specified is designated as of company design: "rudder strut to be Minett-Shields design of universal action, admiralty bronze."

What fun it must have been to deliver *Fleetwood* to her owner's residence on a nice warm spring day in May 1929. It would have been necessary for Bert to open her up a bit, out on the lake, just to be sure she was "in a complete and proper running order."

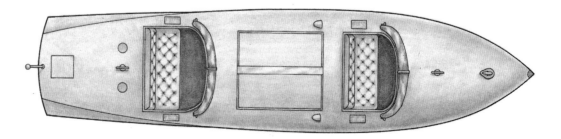

Designer: H. C. (Bert) Minett   Builder: Minett-Shields Co., 1929

CHIPS

is a renovated P-boat—P means that under the Universal Rating Rule, to which she was designed, she rates larger than a Q-boat and smaller than an N-boat. For centuries, men have been trying to devise a rule that would fairly assess the speed-giving elements of a design and allow differing boats to race on equal terms with others. As any student of yacht racing will attest, the search goes on, with the final answer no nearer, nor the route towards it any less in contention. In 1904, Nathanael Herreshoff developed the Universal Rule as an attempt at a simple rating formula that would produce sensible, and fairly-rated, boats. The rule uses length times square root of sail area divided by the cube root of displacement as the standard of judgment as to a boat's potential speed. The formula, even after some later tinkering, was relatively easy to use, and the end result was a numerical rating which roughly corresponded to the boat's waterline length. A boat rating twenty or less was placed in the R-class; one rating twenty-five or less was a Q-boat. To qualify as a P-boat, the rating must be thirty-one or under. So *Chips*, at 51′ 4″ overall and 35′ 11″ on the waterline, and a rating of thirty-one or less, could race against other yachts whose ratings fitted them within the limits of the P-class.

Chips was designed by W. Starling Burgess in 1913 as *Onda III*, and built by the W. Starling Burgess Co. in Marblehead, Massachusetts. The Universal Rule, which produced long-ended, low-sided, heavy displacement boats of above

LOA: 51′ 4″
LWL: 35′ 11″
Beam: 10′ 4″
Draft: 7′ 4″

average beauty, soon gave way to the new International Rule from Europe, and *Chips*, like many other Universal boats, was no longer in the limelight of racing and fell into obscurity. Only a recent major rebuild by her present owner has saved her from the scrapyard.

Having been lucky enough to have sailed on *Chips* after her massive and very successful facelift, I am most grateful for her resurrection. She is exciting, responsive, and beautiful. Her large gaff rig drives her well, and fits her better, I think, than would a marconi sail plan. Her low freeboard and open cockpit puts one close enough to the water to fully appreciate her speed, and tiller steering allows the helmsman to "feel" her motion through the water. It is difficult not to feel a bit holier-than-thou when sailing *Chips* through a fleet of modern sailboats. She has enough presence to draw envious stares from all sides as she romps up the river to her mooring.

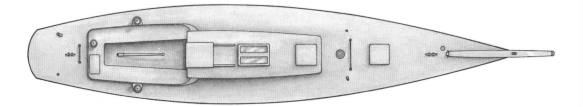

Designer: W. Starling Burgess   Builder: W. Starling Burgess Corp., 1913

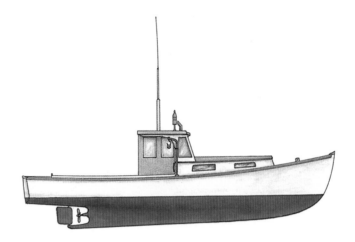

LOBSTERBOATS

come in all sizes and shapes, all degrees of beauty, all colors of the rainbow. Traps are hauled from every sort of craft from flat-bottomed punts rowed by an eager boy to hundred-foot steel vessels captained by resolute men seeking their fortunes and the elusive lobster, along the canyon edges of the outer continental shelf. But when one thinks of the typical Maine lobsterboat, the image is of a swift, low-sided wooden powerboat, perhaps 32 feet long with a low trunk cabin and steering shelter forward, followed by a large open cockpit running aft to the stern.

Fortunately (or unfortunately, depending on one's point of view), the modern lobsterboat fleet is predominated by sturdy fiberglass vessels—wide-beamed, diesel powered, and easily cared-for. I say fortunately, for lobstering is a tough game—long hours, hard work, uncertain pay, cloudy future—and the boats must be up to the tough demands made of them. I say unfortunately, for some of the wooden boats which were the forerunners of these modern work-horses were beautiful examples of functional design and construction, executed by a variety of small boat shops along the coast. These shops were usually one or two man enterprises, and each master builder developed his own designs and construction methods; each successive boat improved on the previous model, and was modified as fishermen's needs changed. "Talking boats" was inevitable when two or more fishermen gathered on the dock and the products of the different boat shops were discussed and argued in infinite detail. Lobsterboats from different regions of the Maine coast developed in distinctly different ways.

Typical lobsterboat dimensions:

LOA:	*34' 0"*
LWL:	*32' 6"*
Beam:	*11' 0"*
Draft:	*3' 0"*

The Jonesport-Beals Island boats were skeg boats, plumb-stemmed with low graceful sheers and shelter cabins with narrow, vertical windows. Farther to the westward, a group of builders on Mount Desert Island were turning out "built-down" hulls with straighter sheers, more rake to the stem, and cabins with a heavier, more "woody" appearance than the Beals boats. Deer Isle-Eggemoggin Reach boats had a slightly different appearance, as did the Muscongus Bay boats. Students of lobsterboat design could identify the area in which a boat was built and real experts could name a boat's builder at a glance.

There was a good mixing of these boat types along the coast. It was not at all unusual for a fisherman from the mid-coast area to travel to Beals to order a new lobsterboat, or for a Maine boat to be built for Massachusetts owners. This promoted development of the lobsterboat as builders up and down the length of the New England coast were exposed to different ideas and details from other shops. It also ensured plenty of "boat talk" on raw and blowy days.

Most wooden lobsterboats were powered by gasoline automotive engines converted for marine use, although the more reliable and expensive diesel was frequently installed. The biggest revolution on lobsterboats came in the 1960s when the hydraulic pothauler replaced the old belt-driven horizontal winch head as the means of pulling the miles and miles of potwarp which lifted the traps from the bottom of the bay to the rail of the boat. The pothauler removed much of the labor from hauling a trap and enabled the fisherman to handle more gear in a shorter time. Since the pothauler lifted the trap to the boat's rail, the need for low freeboard was reduced and boats became higher-sided and more burdensome in order to handle the extra traps now being fished.

Perhaps I have made it sound as though the wooden lobsterboat is gone. This is not quite true. A lot of them are still in use by satisfied owners. A few shops still build an occasional new boat. But the heyday of the wooden fishing fleet is over, and will not return. These photographs will be a long-term record of a vanishing breed.

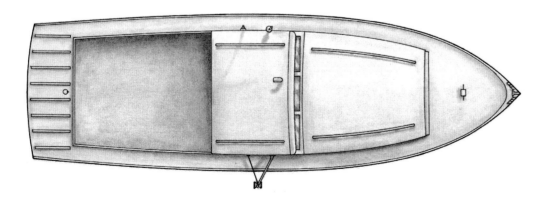

Typical lobsterboat

THE HERRESHOFF 12½

LOA: 15′ 11″
LWL: 12′ 6″
Beam: 5′ 10″
Draft: 2′ 6″

is probably the best small boat design ever drawn. Only sixteen feet long and twelve and one-half feet on the waterline, it has a large comfortable cockpit that can seat four in regal style for an afternoon sail. The boats are seaworthy, good-looking, well built, and long-lasting. They seem much bigger than they are—more like a tiny ship than a small boat. They are fast, fun to sail, and very safe. One can hardly ask for more in a sixteen foot boat.

Designed by Nathanael Herreshoff for use on Buzzards Bay and built by his company, the Herreshoff Manufacturing Co., the first boats of the class came out in 1914. Over the next twenty-five years, hundreds were built, and fleets of them raced on summer weekends in many New England harbors. Generations of sailors grew up sailing 12½s, and now, fifty years later, their children and grandchildren are still sailing the same boats.

The magic of these boats lies not only in their good qualities, but in the beauty of their shape. Handsome from all angles, the shape of the bow is of particular interest. From a wide deck line, the forward sections curve inward quickly to form a waterline with considerable hollow, and continue below water with a trace of reverse curve at the garboard plank. The next time you find a 12½ hauled out, walk around it sighting the subtle curves of the forward

sections from all angles. Nat Herreshoff must have been pleased with this bow, for its shape is echoed in most of his sailboat designs in the years following the debut of the 12½s. There is some evidence that Herreshoff found the inspiration for this shape in a small Bermuda dinghy called *Contest*, presently preserved at the Bermuda Maritime Museum. In any case, it is a gorgeous bit of sculpture, and does much to make the boats so attractive.

12½s have a full deck line, high bilges with the turn well above water, considerable deadrise with a slightly hollow garboard, and seven hundred and fifty pounds of lead ballast bolted to the keel. The high, hard bilges coupled with the goodly chunk of ballast make the boats very stiff, and eliminate the need for side decks to keep out water when heeled. Thus the full beam of the

boat can be utilized in the layout of the cockpit seats, and the high coaming makes a good backrest to lean against. Surely, this has much to do with their continuing appeal—not only are they good trainers for young sailors, but older salts can sit in them in real comfort, unlike so many classes of small boats.

The construction is pure Herreshoff—simplicity combined with elegance and perfect proportion—and the best of materials put together by the finest craftsmen available. As with all Herreshoff boats, virtually every part of the boat was made at the Bristol, Rhode Island, plant. Even the bronze hardware was designed and cast in their own foundry on the premises, accounting for the elegance of the fittings—an elegance not found on boats built using stock hardware and fittings from the marine catalogs.

The boats are so good, and have such a loyal following, that there is a brisk seller's market for them. As soon as one becomes available, there is someone standing by to purchase her, renovate as needed, and enjoy another decade or two of sailing her.

What the 12½ offers (that most modern classes do not) is versatility. You can race around the buoys against other 12½s, you can take your mother out for an afternoon sail, load aboard the whole family for a beach picnic, or with a sleeping bag and a canvas to go over the boom, you can cruise in her for the weekend. One boat I know of was delivered from Massachusetts to mid-coast Maine by a retired seafaring man who simply sailed her from there to here—took about a week.

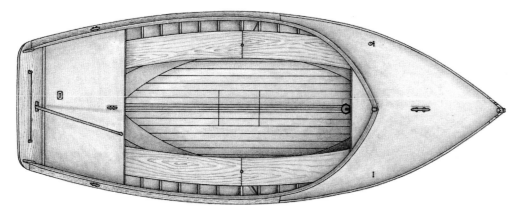

Designer: N. G. Herreshoff   Builder: Herreshoff Mfg. Co., 1914–1943

BABY BOOTLEGGER —the name evokes the era—the roar-

ing twenties, speakeasies, fast cars, fast boats, fast money. The Gold Cup race was the test of fast boats in the twenties, run each year under a set of rules designed to foster speedboats that would also be useful and enjoyable off the race course. Caleb Bragg, wealthy, educated, an automobile racer and flyer, was an officer of the Martin Company, manufacturer of airplanes. In 1923, he won the Gold Cup in a Packard-powered boat named *Packard-Chris Craft*, owned by J. G. Vincent. Bitten by the racing bug, Bragg commissioned a design for a new boat from naval architect George Crouch for the 1924 race. This boat, *Baby Bootlegger*, was built at Nevins' Yard on City Island, N.Y. that spring, and later that summer, with Bragg at the wheel, won the Gold Cup race against a field of nine. She won again in 1925, this time with a Packard replacing the original Hispano-Suiza aircraft engine.

Some time after the 1925 race, *Baby Bootlegger* disappeared from view. She had caught fire, sustained severe damage, and had been given to a scrap dealer. This was the fate of many of the old flyers and few survived. But after a long disappearance and a complex and frustrating period of detective work, a young aficionado of wooden race boats named Mark Mason found *Baby Boot-legger* in 1977. Several years and many thousands of dollars later, a restored *Baby Bootlegger* emerged from the years of decay—looking like new, capturing every heart and every award for excellence at antique and classic boat shows.

LOA: 29' 10"
LWL: 25' 4"
Beam: 5' 11"
Draft: 2' 0"

Powered by a rebuilt Hispano-Suiza V-8, her hull gleaming with many coats of varnish, and wearing her racing number G 5 in gold leaf on each glowing topside, she was ready once more to fulfill her role as the perfect gentleman's runabout and retired champion Gold Cupper.

Much has been written about *Baby Bootlegger*—all of it well-deserved praise for this immaculately restored runabout. The pictures on these pages will show you what all the fuss is about. She is unique: a remarkable boat in design, construction, and performance. To my knowledge, there is not another like her— which is not the normal state of affairs. Most runabout designs were built in multiple copies.

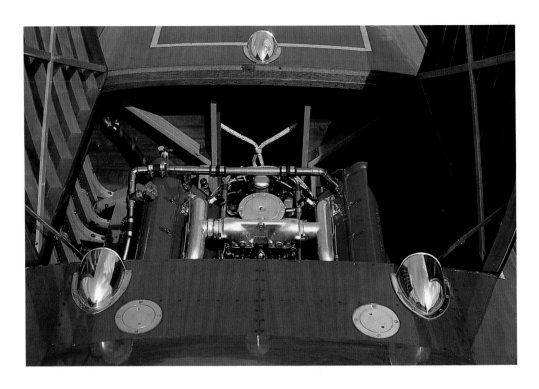

Somehow speed boats fit best in fresh water lakes surrounded by mountains. The salt breezes and boisterous chops found on the sea perimeter are hard on varnish and antique aircraft engines. Pictures of *Baby Bootlegger* are apt to show the softer backgrounds of an Adirondack locale—a placid lake studded with islands, high hills behind, with pines and firs reaching to the lake edge, and the fluffy white high-country clouds reflected in the water's surface. In such a setting, *Baby Bootlegger* and Mark Mason can strut their stuff—the glittering speed which converts a mahogany tube into a projectile, travelling across the surface at 50 or 60 miles per hour; yet not a frightening ride, but one filled with fun and exhilaration. A gentleman's runabout with her gentleman aboard, enjoying the flight.

When not in use, *Baby Bootlegger* is hoisted clear of the water, parked in her own boathouse built out over the lake, suspended safely inside her slip. It makes one wonder what her true element really is . . . water? air?

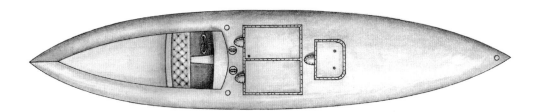

Designer: George Crouch   Builder: Henry B. Nevins Inc., 1924

BELLE AVENTURE

is Fife designed and Fife built. Every once in a while, families like the Fifes (and the Herreshoffs) with special talent in yacht design will emerge head and shoulders above the pack, illuminating the yachting scene for years to come. At Fairlie, in western Scotland, the first William Fife started designing and building boats early in the nineteenth century. His son, also William, took over the business in 1839. He designed and built many well-known yachts, his fame growing for more than forty years until 1881, when he retired and handed over the reins and the reputation to his son, also William. This third William Fife, of course, is the one we know most about, and whose yachts are most familiar to us. He had a remarkable career, designing and building yachts from 1876 until 1940, when the outbreak of World War II stopped yacht building at Fairlie. Much of his output was in the meter racing classes—6s, 8s, 12s, and the larger 23-meter class. He also designed several gorgeous large schooners—*Cicely* and *Suzanne* among them—and a series of Shamrocks for Sir Thomas Lipton as challengers for the America's Cup. *Shamrock III*, designed in 1903, was a fine looking boat, and a marvelous piece of engineering. She had the misfortune to be matched against Herreshoff's *Reliance*, an unbeatable boat and also an engineering masterpiece.

LOA: 85′ 0″
LWL: 62′ 0″
Beam: 17′ 2″
Draft: 10′ 7″

Belle Aventure, a product of Fife's later years, was designed and built at the William Fife and Sons yard at Fairlie, on the Firth of Clyde. Originally named *Eileen* and built for Louis Fulton, she, like most large yachts, had a checkered career. Enjoying the good years with good owners, she suffered through the bad times when money and care were in short supply. Badly in need of a refit in 1979, she was sailed from Malta home to the Clyde and underwent a two year refurbishing which brought her back to near perfection. Since that time, she has been a splendid example of the large, privately owned, older yacht that spends its time between the Mediterranean and the Caribbean, with an occasional visit north to England or to America. Serving as vacation home for her owner and perhaps chartering occasionally to help earn her keep, she delights all who sail aboard her. Her teak-panelled staterooms, curved stairs leading below, and her general feel of luxury and beauty both alow and aloft remind us of an earlier standard of comfort afloat.

So here is *Belle Aventure*—an eighty-five-foot-long ketch from another time and place. The time was 1929, the place Fairlie, Scotland. She is so large and so beautiful that we tend to think of her as something supernatural, a special once-in-a-lifetime object. But in reality, yachts of this size and calibre were not unusual at all—not in 1929, in England and Scotland. Indeed, eighty-five footers and larger were almost the norm. The most unusual thing about *Belle Aventure* is that she is still with us.

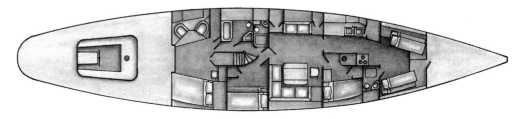

Designer: William Fife   Builder: William Fife & Sons, 1929

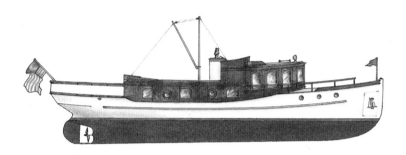

KIYI —fifty feet of splendid old-fashioned powerboat from Seattle, Washington. No streamlining, no fish-eye windows, no Italian styling; just a long, narrow, easily-driven hull with the large deckhouse and forward pilothouse that is almost standard on powerboats from the damp, misty, and cool coastal waters of the Pacific Northwest. The climate dictates the layout; big cockpits and wide-open deck areas are not needed—shelter is the thing. Where the sun is a scarce commodity, a roof overhead is comforting.

LOA: 50′ 0″
LWL: 46′ 10″
Beam: 10′ 4″
Draft: 3′ 3″

As the photographs show, she has a style which speaks of an earlier era, and indeed she was built in 1926. Designed by Leigh Coolidge and built by Schertzer Brothers on Lake Union, Seattle, she has an elegance that will always appeal. Her long waterline and narrow beam make for an easily-driven hull. Originally powered by a Hall-Scott 100-horsepower gasoline engine, she now has a Chrysler Royal straight eight. Modest horsepower for a fifty footer, but ample for her needs.

Her pilothouse provides an enclosed steering station; a folding table here converts the area for dining at anchor. On nice days, or in tight maneuvering situations, the helmsman can operate *Kiyi* from the open bridge on top of the cabin trunk just aft of the pilothouse. An upright oval funnel gives a big-boat touch to her looks, as well as providing a hiding place for the stove pipe from the cabin heater. Aft of the funnel is a low mast with boom, useful for launching the tender from its chocks atop the deckhouse.

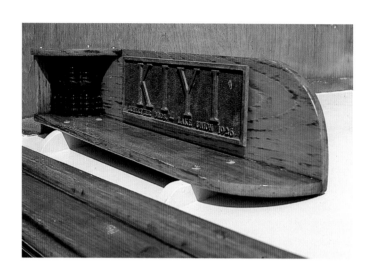

Moving towards the stern, we come to the open aft-deck with deck chairs enclosed by the rail stanchions and canvas dodger. This is a similar but smaller edition of *Canim*'s lounge area. As with many Pacific powerboats, *Kiyi* has a lovely elliptical "steamboat" stern. Why is such a handsome ending for a hull seen so seldom on the East Coast?

Kiyi has been owned for a number of years by Tom and Patti Henderson of Bainbridge Island, Washington. Their care and concern for *Kiyi*'s well-being is immediately evident, as is the enjoyment which her stewardship brings to them. Sometimes one hears owners of older vessels complain that the boat owns them, that they are slaves to her care. Not the Hendersons—rather, I sense that being custodians to her preservation is a source of pleasure and pride.

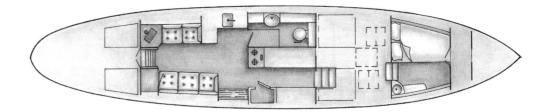

Designer: Leigh Coolidge   Builder: Schertzer Bros., 1926

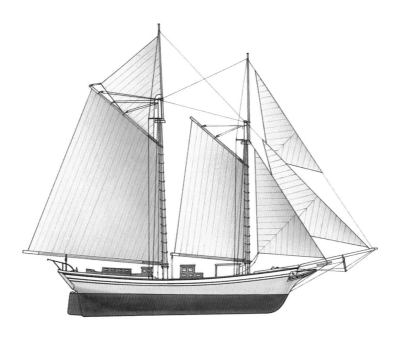

HERITAGE

is a working girl. A ninety-three foot coasting schooner, she carries passengers during the four months of warm weather along the Maine coast, voyaging for a week at a time, returning to her home port of Rockland on Saturdays, and setting sail again with a new cargo of passengers on Monday mornings. Designed and built by her owners Doug and Linda Lee, with help from the Lees' partner John Foss, she joined the growing schooner fleet in the spring of 1983. Maine is one of the few areas left with a working sailing fleet, and during summer months Tuesday is "schooner day" on Eggemoggin Reach—the day we are most apt to see a string of schooners reaching by in the afternoon sou'wester. It's a grand sight, this procession of large sailing vessels booming by, loaded with eager vacationers soaking up the pleasures of the down-East coast.

Most of the schooners are old ones—the *Lewis R. French* and *Stephen Taber* for instance were built in 1871. They are a mixed lot; some, like the *Taber* and the *Mattie*, started life as coasting schooners making their living carrying any and all cargos up and down the eastern coast. Others, like the *Adventure* and *American Eagle*, were fishing vessels—*Adventure* was a Gloucester highliner for many years. Some came from Delaware Bay—like the *Isaac H. Evans* and the *J. & E. Riggin*—where they dredged for oysters before becoming passenger carriers. But as traditional uses for large wooden craft faded, these schooners were bought up and put into the summer cruise business.

LOA: 93' 0"
LWL: 80' 2"
Beam: 24' 0"
Draft: 8' 4"

As these cruises became more popular in the 1960s and 1970s, a few schooners were built new for the trade. The *Mary Day* was launched in 1962, the *Harvey Gamage* in 1973. The Lees and John Foss started out owning old vessels—the *Isaac H. Evans* and *Lewis R. French*—and spent much of each winter repairing and renovating them. When the idea of building a new schooner came to the forefront, they already had a place to do it: the North End Shipyard in Rockland, which they had built up as a base for the repair of their own schooners, and when time permitted, other schooners in the fleet. In the fall of 1979, the decision had been made and the building process started. The schooner was worked on during the fall and winter months for four years until she was launched on April 16, 1983.

The scene on launching day was reminiscent of another era, when large wooden ships were being built on a regular basis along the Maine coast. Hundreds of friends, well-wishers, schooner freaks, and I suppose a few sceptics descended on North End Shipyard on a cold, rainy morning. *Heritage*, looking very fine in her off-white topsides with red, white, and blue stripes along her waist, waited for the tide on the big railway. Her descent into the cold waters of Rockland Harbor was so sedate that it was difficult to know the actual moment when her keel left the blocks. But suddenly she was afloat and moving towards

the dock. Linda and Doug and John looked nonchalant, but pleased. The rest of us were a bit overwhelmed by the magnitude of the accomplishment, and half-frozen by the April North Atlantic weather.

Building a vessel of this size is a monumental job: four years of winter work, 100,000 board feet of lumber most of which was specially cut and milled for the job, plus all the hundreds of items necessary to finish the ship, the thousands of details to be decided and completed. The launching of *Heritage*, the first large new vessel from North End Shipyard, put the yard on the map as the home of big schooners, whether old ones in need of repair, or new ones to be built. Rockland was a shipbuilding town again.

Every summer since 1983, *Heritage* is one of the fine sights of the mid-coast region of Maine. Like her ancestors, this coasting schooner puts into every harbor, cove, or island anchorage where business calls. Where the cargos used to be lumber, granite, pulp wood, casks of lime, or holds full of cobblestones, now the payload is passengers, anxious to savor the sights and sounds of the summer coast, taste the fog and the lobster stew, visit the villages and the empty anchorages of the offshore islands. To see her slipping through the narrow passages between Stonington and Isle au Haut, with her topsails showing above the island spruces, is to glimpse a vision of this coast a century ago.

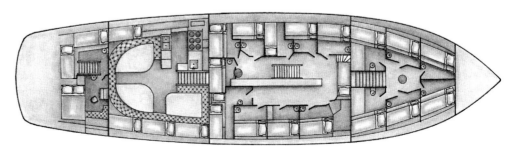

Designer: Doug and Linda Lee   Builder: North End Shipyard, 1983

PEAPODS

—in the marine world the name refers to boats, not vegetables. Fourteen to eighteen feet long, double-ended, usually with identical bow and stern, peapods were the common small rowing craft of the Maine coast in the late nineteenth century. If you look at a well filled out peapod, fresh off the vine, you will have an idea of the shape of the boats, and why they were so named.

Howard Chapelle, the noted marine historian and genealogist of boat types, states that peapods developed about 1870 on the island of North Haven, Maine. Unlike most boat types, they do not seem to have evolved from an earlier model, but rather are an amalgam of many double-ended forerunners— whaleboats, No Man's Land boats, and others. John Gardner, another student of boat types and boat development, seems to agree with Chapelle, but says that the Indian canoe also influenced the early builders of 'pods. In any case, the boats became popular because of their load-carrying ability in rough water, their ease of rowing, and their stability. Heavily-built, the early 'pods made fine little workboats for tending lobster traps and other alongshore jobs. In the late 1800s, a man only fished forty or fifty lobster pots, and his string of traps was set in a limited area. For lobstering, the boats were rowed standing up with the oarsman facing forward to spot his buoys, and the oarlocks were extended several inches above the gunwales to make rowing easier. The traps were hauled by hand, with one foot on the gunwale, and the stability of the boats was

Typical peapod dimensions:

LOA: *13' 6"*
LWL: *11' 6"*
Beam: *4' 6"*
Draft: *0' 7"*

such that the seventy-five pound trap could be brought in over the gunwale safely, even in choppy water. Early peapods were often lapstrake, but carvel planking became more popular as time went on. A small spritsail often assisted the rower downwind.

Most of the peapods shown on these pages are built by Jim Steele, only a few of the more than one hundred built by Jim over the past twenty-five years for

use as recreational rowboats and yacht tenders. Peapods have made such a comeback in recent years that shops such as Jim's turn them out on a regular basis for a small but steady clientele who like their looks and handling qualities, and are cognizant of their link with the past.

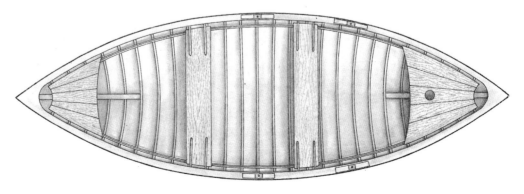

Typical peapod

GLEAM

—the name comes from a line of poetry by Tennyson—"follow, follow, follow the gleam." Since her launching in 1937, many competitors have had occasion to "follow the *Gleam*" around the racecourse. Built to the 12-meter class for racing in Long Island Sound, she still frequents those waters, and the great yachting center of Newport, Rhode Island. More than fifty years old now, she turns heads whenever she is in sight.

And with good reason. This sixty-eight foot racing sloop, with her gleaming varnished trim and polished brass hardware, takes us back in time to yachting's glory days.

Today's perception of a 12-meter is a utilitarian metal racing boat, studded with winches, manned by athletic giants in oilskins, and serviced by an array of shoreside support groups—riggers, sailmakers, financiers, psychologists, and public-relations men. Since 1958, 12-meters have been the class chosen to race for the America's Cup; prior to that, the America's Cup was raced for in much larger boats. But the 12-meter class, starting back in the early days of this century, once produced truly lovely racing yachts with interior accommodations to house their crews. The 12-meters first became very popular in Europe; there was an active fleet in England in the twenties and thirties which gave some good racing for the owners. Around 1930, with the importation of several boats from abroad, the US fleet began to grow, and regular racing took place on Long

LOA:	68′ 0″
LWL:	45′ 2″
Beam:	12′ 0″
Draft:	8′ 9″

Island Sound. In 1935 Clinton Crane designed *Seven Seas* for Van Merle-Smith, and she proved to be a very successful 12-meter. The next year, Merle-Smith loaned *Seven Seas* to Crane, in order to persuade him to join the fun and have a 12-meter of his own. Crane, an ardent yachtsman, did well racing her, and indeed the next year, 1937, designed *Gleam* and had her built for his own use by the H. B. Nevins Co. of City Island, New York. In 1938 Olin Stephens was asked to design *Nyala* and *Northern Light*, and in 1939 Stephens drew up *Vim*, perhaps the most successful 12-meter of all time, for Harold Vanderbilt. Vanderbilt took *Vim* abroad and did very well racing against the European 12s.

Clinton Crane, designer and first owner of *Gleam*, was a most interesting man. A year after the completion of his studies in naval architecture, he was offered the commission to design and supervise building of a 126 foot waterline steam auxiliary yacht, rigged as a brigantine. This is not an inconsiderable undertaking for a very young man just out of engineering school, but he proceeded to do the job and *Aloha*, a handsome and successful vessel, was the result. He also became interested and active in early powerboat racing, and designed a series of boats to race for the Harmsworth Trophy. After eighteen years as a naval architect, he gave it up, became president of the St. Joseph Lead Co., and only returned to boat designing late in life, as a hobby.

Starting again in 1922, he designed racing yachts for the next fifteen years. One of the highlights of this career must have been the design of *Weetamoe*, a J-boat contender for the 1930 American Cup races. While *Enterprise* was chosen over *Weetamoe* to defend the Cup, many consider *Weetamoe* to have been the faster boat.

Reading Clinton Crane's yachting memoirs, one gets the strong impression that *Gleam* was the favorite of all his designs. She certainly offered him much good racing and cruising, and her continuing presence on today's yachting scene is a tribute to Crane and the craftsmen of the Nevins Co. who built her more than fifty years ago.

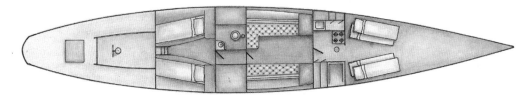

Designer: Clinton Crane   Builder: Henry B. Nevins Inc., 1937

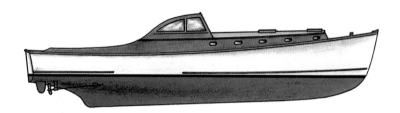

JERICHO

a forty-three foot Maine coast powerboat, was named for the lovely bay which lies between Isle au Haut and Mount Desert Island, and not for the ancient town whose walls came tumbling down. Jericho Bay is the lower extension of Blue Hill Bay, one of the prettiest stretches of water anywhere, with the mountains of Mount Desert rising to the east, the round knob of Blue Hill to the north, and the spruce-clad slopes of Isle au Haut (Champlain's High Island) rising out of the sea and enclosing the bay on its western side.

Jericho is a pleasure boat built on the lines of working lobsterboats, a type which the boating press has recently begun calling "lobsteryachts." The name may be new, but the idea of using lobsterboat hulls for pleasure purposes is not; I suspect that early builders of powered lobsterboats were asked to deliver pleasure boat versions almost from the beginning. Until recently, the type was indigenous to the New England coast, but the virtues of these boats are beginning to be known to a wider audience, and the down-East hull is in evidence almost everywhere along the U. S. coast, and even in Bermuda and the Caribbean.

Jericho was built in 1956 by Raymond Bunker and Ralph Ellis, two lobster-boat builders who combined to form the firm of Bunker & Ellis. Located on the island of Mount Desert, their shop produced boats for the local fishing fleet working the cold, deep waters surrounding the island. But Mount Desert was also the summer home for a large number of well-to-do folks who needed

LOA:	42′ 11″
LWL:	40′ 6″
Beam:	11′ 9″
Draft:	3′ 4″

a good power launch to attend to all the water-borne tasks involved in island living—ferry service, picnics, or transporting groceries. Bunker & Ellis began to fill this demand with a succession of practical, good-looking boats based on their fishing boat models, but gussied up a bit with varnished mahogany cabins and trim. Nearly all these boats have bunks, a head, and a galley below, and either single or twin gasoline engines. Some have hard-top shelters over the bridge, but most, like *Jericho*, are built with an open bridge deck with windshield, and a canvas cover that can be deployed to shelter the helmsman from excessive sun or rain. The boats range in size from about thirty feet to forty-five feet overall.

Raymond and Ralph turned out a great many of these superior boats, all bearing certain trademark features identifying them as products of the Bunker & Ellis shop. A low, graceful sheer, narrow beam, the hull painted white with a black boot top, and varnished mahogany deck structures—all say "Bunker & Ellis." Many people, myself among them, think *Jericho* is the handsomest of all. A sail across Jericho Bay on a summer afternoon towards Mount Desert almost always results in the happy sight of one or more Bunker & Ellis boats going about their duties—hosting a picnic or an afternoon pleasure cruise, or just waiting on the mooring for the next call. Continuing your sail up Western Way to Northeast Harbor, you will pass a number of these sweet powerboats, looking right at home in their grand surroundings.

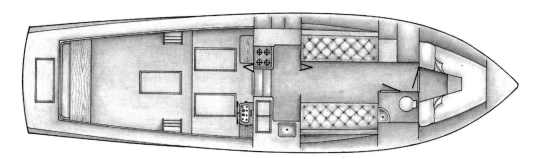

Designer: Bunker & Ellis   Builder: Bunker & Ellis, 1956

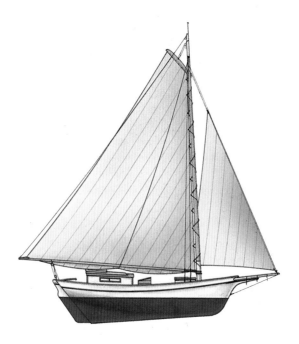

UNITY B

sails on a fiercely blue sea, the water so clear that it appears insubstantial and unable to support the weight of the sloop. The hull seems suspended in air, above the water. The sun here is a force—white-hot, blinding, a series of scintillating flashes on the rough sea surface. The breeze is from the east, and an endless procession of trade-wind clouds marches down the wind, dappling the sky above the boat. The place is Grassy Creek Cay, just off the south end of the Andros chain in the Bahamas. These are *Unity B*'s home waters.

The man on the boat squints in the sun's glare. Alfred Bain is her owner, skipper, and builder. She is the tool by which he earns his living, drawing his sustenance from the sea. Bain is seventy now, and fishes for conch near Grassy Creek Cay with a crew of three other men. Conch are caught by hooking them off the bottom with a long-handled two-pronged conch hook, known as a grabber, and by skin diving from a small dinghy. A conch trip may take a month: two weeks loading *Unity B* with up to three thousand conchs, a couple of days sail to market at Nassau with a stop at Bain's home, Lisbon Creek, on the way, a week or more in Nassau hawking the conch off the boat to passersby, and a couple of days home to Lisbon Creek to prepare for the next trip. Although she is one of the few left, *Unity B* does this entirely under sail—she has no engine.

Alfred Bain built *Unity B* in 1950 at Lisbon Creek on Mangrove Cay. "I guess I learned to build boats from inheritance. Our forefathers and everybody at

LOA: 36' 0"
LWL: 31' 9"
Beam: 12' 0"
Draft: 4' 10"

Lisbon Creek were boatbuilders." *Unity B* is a typical, though perhaps more handsome than average, Bahamian sloop, a type whose numbers are decreasing, and whose species almost certainly is endangered. Built mostly of local Andros woods, she has the graceful sheer and beautifully modeled transom stern which characterize the best of the Bahamian sloops. The mast is far forward, and the mainsail is the principal sail—the long overhanging boom and heavily roached loose-footed sail provide a lot of area for light air days. When it blows up, the sail is quickly reefed. The jib is small, setting to the end of the bowsprit, and it too is reefed as needed, simply by tying up the clew and attaching the sheet higher up the leech.

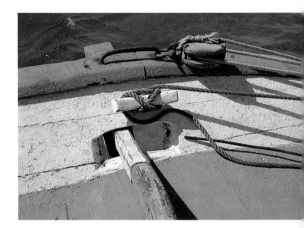

Unity B has a wet-well, in which conch and fish can be kept alive while on the way to distant markets. Aft there is a small cabin house under which the crew sleeps. Cooking is done on deck in a cookbox. The deck is cluttered with grabbers, glass-bottomed buckets for spotting conchs, a freshwater barrel, and anchors. As conchs are caught, a hole is punched in their shells and they are tied together in groups of five. Thrown overboard in shallow water, they are kept alive until ready to be transported to Nassau.

In most parts of the Bahamas, the modern world has intruded pretty heavily on the old pace of life. Nassau, and most of the other islands, are regularly invaded by tourists seeking the old-world, quiet scenes, and by their seeking, making them scarce. Planes and cruise ships regularly arrive and depart with new crowds of people. So it is unusual to find an operation such as Alfred Bain and his *Unity B* still fishing in the old way, under sail—living life at five knots instead of fifty, or five hundred.

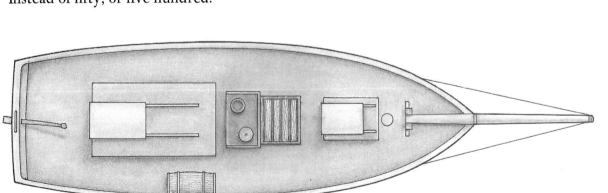

Designer: Alfred Bain   Builder: Alfred Bain, 1950

BEETLE CATS

must hold some kind of longevity record—oldest one-design class in continuous production—or something of the sort. They must also hold a record for family loyalty to one boat, as many families now have grandchildren (perhaps even great-grands) sailing boats first purchased by Grandpa and Grandma. Whatever the records, it is a heart-warming story of a wooden boat defying and defeating the passage of time, the boatbuilding revolution from wood to fiberglass, and changes in sailing technology. A 1988 Beetle Cat looks the same as a 1930, or a 1950, Beetle Cat. The sail will be Dacron instead of canvas, the running rigging synthetic instead of natural manila fiber, the screws holding the planks to the frames are now bronze instead of galvanized iron, but the hull is still the same shape, the planking still cedar over oak frames, the deck still canvas covered. Sitting on the floorboards, staring up at the luff of the gaff mainsail, the coaming will still hit the same place on your shoulder blade, the twinge reminding you of childhood voyages, the glare from the sail deepening the squint lines around the eyes started many years ago by an earlier sail, a long-ago sun.

John Beetle of New Bedford, Massachusetts, built the first boats for his children in 1920. Beetle was a well-known builder of whaleboats, big double-ended rowing craft which were lowered from the davits of whaleships to pursue the huge cetaceans for their oil. The little catboats caught the fancy of the local

LOA: 12' 4"
LWL: 11' 6"
Beam: 6' 1"
Draft: 0' 7"

yachtsmen, and fleets sprang up around Cape Cod and Buzzards Bay. Sixty years later, there are fleets all over New England.

Good boats invariably prosper and benefit from the interest of good men. In the Beetle Cat story, there are two who stand out: Waldo Howland, ever the friend and champion of wooden boats, and Leo Telesmanick. Leo went to work for the Beetle family, and after a five year apprenticeship was put in charge of building the Beetle Cats. This was in 1936. World War II put a stop to the building of pleasure boats and Leo went to work for the Palmer Scott Co. constructing boats for the war effort. In 1946 the Beetle Cat business was sold by the Beetle family to Waldo Howland, owner of the Concordia Co. Waldo, knowing a good man and a good boat when he saw one, arranged for Leo to continue

building Beetle Cats at Palmer Scott. In 1960 the whole operation (including Leo) was moved to Smith Neck, South Dartmouth, across the harbor from the Concordia Co. yard, and it has been there ever since. Leo retired in 1983, after fifty-three years of boatbuilding, but Beetle Cats are still going strong. Thousands have been built and thousands are still in use. Waldo, in his quiet way, has been a great proponent and promoter of Beetle Cats, and has ensured the facilities and ongoing interest, enabling such a project to flourish. In 1969, Waldo retired and sold the Concordia Company, but subsequent owners continue the tradition of building Beetles.

Whenever I see a fleet of Beetles racing, I always think of a flock of ducks—Old Squaws perhaps—playful and perky, splashing about with immense good cheer and an unconscious feeling of invincibility.

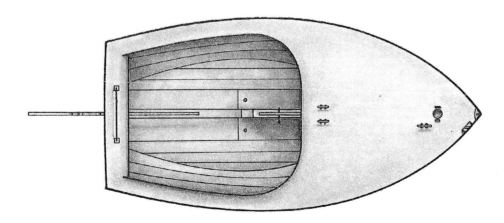

Designer: John Beetle   Builder: Concordia Co., 1930 to present

VOYAGER

and her near-sister *Tarbaby* are fifty foot Alden schooners. Nine boats were built to this design, number 390, including one, *Rogue*, later *Venturer*, for John Alden himself. Alden was a great hand to have one of his designs built, use her for a while to get to know her, then resell the boat and move on to another.

Several of the 390s were built by C. A. Morse & Son of Thomaston, Maine, in 1929 and 1930. The Morse yard built a great many of Alden's designs, and it is recorded that the Morse-built *Zaida II*, another 390, was completed for the sum of $4800, an indication of how far a dollar stretched in those days.

This particular hull design could be called early Alden classic—a husky, heavy displacement hull with full bilges, nicely raked elliptical stern, and a heavily knuckled stem profile. John Alden was an admirer of the Gloucester fishing schooner type, and his early designs for offshore cruising and racing mirror this admiration. This is not to say that the boats were miniatures of Gloucester schooners, but the influence is there. The 390-class lines were drawn by Aage Nielsen, at the time one of Alden's house designers who later became well known in his own right, albeit for designing a different type of boat.

The John Alden office was headquarters for schooners in the 1920s and 1930s —they must have designed more of them than anyone else. It is hard to deny the appeal of the schooner rig. On an appropriate hull, no rig looks better or

LOA: 50' 1"
LWL: 39' 10"
Beam: 14' 3"
Draft: 7' 2"

Voyager

Tarbaby

appeals more to the romantic in any sailor. The rig makes a lot of sense for really large hulls; the sail plan can be reduced to a number of relatively small sail units for easier handling. It also has the advantage of simplicity—the short, solid spars do not need high-tech rigging and fittings for proper staying. Many people, however, prefer looking at the other fellow's schooner to owning one themselves. The schooner's drawbacks are undeniable: lots of windage, miles of rigging, and mediocre ability to windward.

Tarbaby

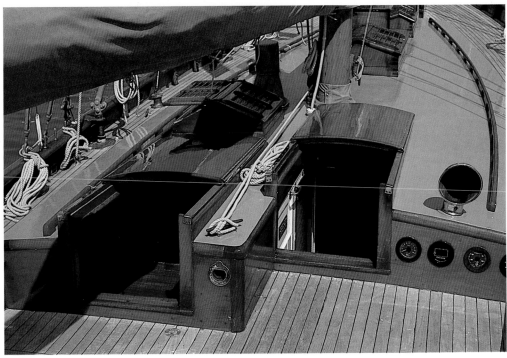

Tarbaby

Voyager

Voyager

Tarbaby

The original sail plan for the 390 schooners was the traditional gaff-headed plan with main topsail. *Voyager* still has this rig. *Tarbaby* has been changed to a staysail schooner, in which the gaff foresail is replaced by a club-footed staysail and a large fisherman staysail, thus filling the space between the two masts. Her mainsail was changed from gaff to marconi.

Tarbaby, seen in these photographs, is the original boat built by Morse in 1929. *Voyager* is not. When Peter Phillipps bought *Voyager* in 1962, she was showing her age, and leaked—a lot. Ten years of expensive repairs never cured the leaking, and wanting to make long offshore voyages, he decided to build a new hull, copying the old one, and using whatever was salvageable from the original boat. This was done at the Smith & Rhuland yard in Lunenburg, Nova Scotia. The old iron ballast keel, deck fittings, chain plates, tanks, anchors, pumps, steering gear, and rig were transferred to the new hull. Phillipps, in an article for WoodenBoat Magazine, describes the process, and the result, a new *Voyager* with much of the old boat incorporated into her, has proved entirely satisfactory.

Carl Sherman, owner of *Tarbaby* since 1973, has pursued a program of restoration and maintenance, bringing her to the point where she has won numerous awards for best boat at various antique and classic boat shows. Two different approaches to dealing with a much-loved older boat, and both approaches yielding estimable results.

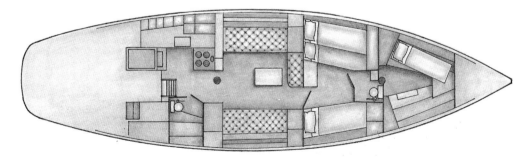

Designer: John Alden Co.   Builder: Chas. A. Morse & Sons, 1929

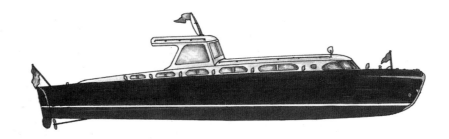

THUNDERBIRD

is the biggest, the heaviest, the fastest mahogany speedboat you are ever apt to see. Most adjectives which describe her end in *est*. She even has the biggest, shiniest (see what I mean) stainless steel cabin this side of an Amtrak coach. A stainless steel cabin!

One nice thing about *Thunderbird*, built in 1939, is that she suits her home waters to a T. T for Tahoe. Lake Tahoe has been her home for most of her life. Tahoe is a mountain lake, elevation 6500 feet, on the border of California and Nevada. Mountain peaks surround the lake and on its shores summer a host of speedboat enthusiasts; it is estimated by Peter Spectre, a journalist specializing in the boating scene, that there may be more than five hundred mahogany speedboats in residence at Tahoe. That's a lot of speedboats for a lake twenty-five miles long. Most of the owners of these boats have enough money to take their enthusiasms seriously. One collector owns thirty-nine; that's seriously.

The flashiest, most visible of all is *Thunderbird*. Also the most audible. When she cranks up her twin 1000-horsepower Allison aircraft engines, it is evident that she is in the area. *Thunderbird* was once owned by Bill Harrah, well-known casino operator, and well-known collector of fast things—fast cars, fast motorcycles, fast boats. It was he who installed the Allisons to get her speed up to 70 knots. He also altered her interior to accommodate a four table, plush-lined cocktail lounge with mirrored bulkheads.

LOA: 55′ 0″
LWL: 52′ 9″
Beam: 11′ 10″
Draft: 2′ 7″

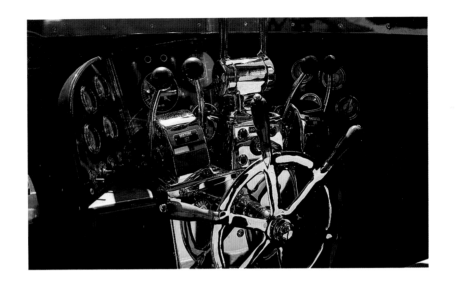

This highly unusual vessel was conceived by the dean of speedboat designers, John Hacker. She really is a marvel when you consider the problems involved in making a boat of this size (fifty-five feet) and weight (sixteen tons) move at high speed. She was built by the Huskin Boatbuilding Co. in Bay City, Michigan. *Thunderbird* has a fuel capacity of 300 gallons of aviation gas, which allows her two circumnavigations of Lake Tahoe at almost full-bore. Designed to flabbergast, she fulfills her mission perfectly—to be the mostest mahogany speedboat on the lake.

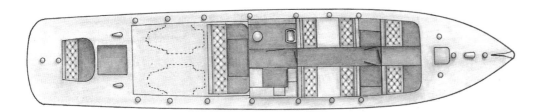

Designer: John Hacker   Builder: Huskin Boatbuilding Co., 1939

THE DARK HARBOR 20s

are a racing class used exclusively at the island of Islesboro on the Maine coast. This large island is located in Penobscot Bay, just a few miles northeast of Camden, where there has been a large summer colony since before the turn of the century concentrated around the shores of Dark Harbor. Sailboat racing has always been one of the favored summer sports.

Early in the 1900s, racing on Islesboro was done in Dark Harbor 12s and 17s, handsome gaff-rigged sloops designed by Crowninshield. As these boats got older and more difficult to maintain, it was decided to have a new class. In 1935 Olin Stephens, then a young man and fledgling yacht designer, was commissioned to do the design and six boats were built at Lawley's yard. They proved to be excellent—both faster and more comfortable than the 17s. More boats were ordered until the class grew to a total of twenty-one.

Dark Harbor 20s are long-ended, with a short fin keel. The sail plan is a conventional marconi sloop, with the headstay going three-quarters of the way to the masthead (what is now called a fractional rig). A small rectangular cuddy cabin provides limited shelter below and a dry place to keep sails, picnic baskets, and small children. Regular afternoon racing has long been an established event at Dark Harbor, and it is a fine sight on a breezy summer day to see the fleet tearing around the racing buoys, multicolored spinnakers flying on the downwind legs, while white spray flies on the beats to windward.

LOA: 30′ 2″
LWL: 20′ 0″
Beam: 6′ 9″
Draft: 4′ 1″

The most remarkable thing about these boats is that after fifty years of racing they are still the boat of choice at Dark Harbor. The Islesboro summer community could safely be called a conservative group; rushing out to buy the latest in go-fast racing sloops just isn't high on the priority list. There is no pressure to compete with nearby yacht clubs in modern racers and so the old boats, as much a part of the summer scene as the turn-of-the-century summer cottages and morning tennis games, are cherished for their link to older generations and bygone summer memories.

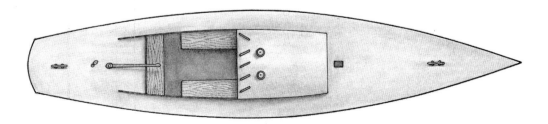

Designer: Sparkman & Stephens   Builder: Geo. Lawley & Son, 1935–36

ANNIE

a lovely twenty-four foot double-ended yawl designed by Fenwick Williams, is a child of the Great Depression. Drawn in 1932, her design was an attempt to keep yacht building alive in those dark financial days by dramatically reducing the scale of a typical cruising boat. Fenwick Williams at the time was one of a most able group of naval architects working at the office of John G. Alden Co. in Boston. Before the 1929 crash, a fifty foot yacht was thought to be none too big for cruising. In 1932, Williams knew that a yacht even twenty-four feet long might be too large for budgets of the day.

LOA: 24′ 0″
LWL: 21′ 4″
Beam: 8′ 8″
Draft: 3′ 10″

Fenwick Williams is a designer whose talents greatly exceed his fame. *Annie* is a tribute to this talent—only yacht designers know how difficult it is to make a small chunky hull look graceful, how difficult to blend all elements into a harmonious whole when the boat has high freeboard, great beam, and full sections. *Annie* is a lot of boat for twenty-four feet overall, yet in the water under sail, she looks as graceful as a gull.

There are some distinctive and unusual features about *Annie*. The cabin trunk is short enough that a small (6′ 8″) tender can be stowed crosswise aft of the mainmast. Very few twenty-four footers can carry their dinghy on deck. The yawl rig is not often seen on so small a boat, but was no doubt specified in part to give the impression that she is larger. Her steering is unusual in that a bent shaft passes through the sternpost and the mizzenmast, and works in a slot in the upper part of the rudder. Rotating the shaft causes the rudder to turn.

Apparently only two boats were built to these plans back in the thirties, indicating the true depth of the Depression. But the attractiveness of the design was demonstrated nearly fifty years after its conception when Art Brendze of Arundel Shipyard in Kennebunkport, Maine, was motivated to build *Annie* on speculation. Traditionally constructed with cedar planking on oak frames, and bronze fastenings, she is a beautiful piece of work. The rig is just as Fenwick Williams drew it back in 1932—a high-peaked gaff mainsail, small leg-o-mut-

ton mizzen, and self-tending jib with club. Dacron sails, of course, replace the canvas that would have been used fifty years earlier, but otherwise the rigging is traditional and simple. Below decks, there is an astonishing six feet of head-room under the house, and six foot four inches under the companionway slide. Brendze made some changes to the original accommodations, so that there is a double berth forward, as well as two settee berths, and a small galley. A lot of space for such a little boat.

Ownerless, and an orphan at launching time, she was named *Annie*. Her dinghy, of course, was named *Sandy*.

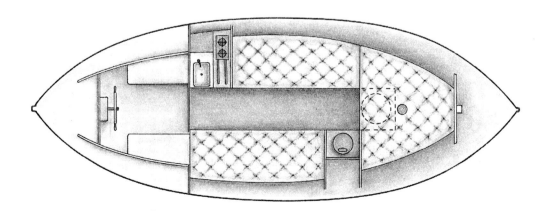

Designer: Fenwick Williams   Builder: Arundel Shipyard, 1980

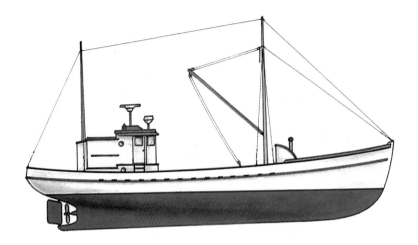

SARDINE CARRIERS are the queens of the Maine fishing fleet.

These are good sized boats, sixty feet and up in length, and are used to move sardines, or small herring, from the point of capture to the factory where the fish are processed and placed head-to-tail into cans. The fish may have to be moved a hundred miles or more, although most of the trips are considerably shorter.

The evolution of the sardine carrier is a long one, starting with thirty-foot sail-powered "carryaway" boats and larger schooners in the late nineteenth century. About 1900, the internal combustion engine made its appearance in the fleet. Perishable cargos, such as sardines, were a big incentive to switch to mechanical power, and the sailing vessels were soon converted into propeller-driven carriers. As the power plants improved and became larger, the boats became longer and more capacious. A typical vessel of the early 1900s would have been sixty feet long with thirteen foot beam. In the 1950s, a typical carrier measured seventy to eighty feet long with seventeen foot beam, and had nearly double the carrying capacity of the earlier vessels. Many, although by no means all, were double-enders, dictated by the need for easily-driven shapes when both light and loaded. For the same reason, the boats were long and lean, and consequently often very beautiful.

"Pauline", a typical sardine carrier:

LOA:	*83′ 7″*
LWL:	*72′ 3″*
Beam:	*18′ 0″*
Draft:	*5′ 0″*

Herring are usually caught at night, either in fish weirs along the shores, or by seining, when the fish are circled by long nets that can be pursed at the bottom to contain the fish. After capture, the herring are transferred from the seine or weir into the hold of the carrier by a fish pump. During this process, the fish are scaled and the scales saved for use in making cosmetics and lipstick. As soon as the carrier is loaded, she heads for her factory dock to unload the fish for immediate processing. If fish are plentiful, she may be making almost continuous trips during the herring run and the factory will be working double shifts.

The sardine industry has a long history of fluctuating prosperity and is presently in a lengthy decline. The last carriers were built in the 1950s, and the size of the present fleet is smaller than ever as factories close and demand for the product declines. But the two dozen or so carriers that still transport sardines along Maine's indented coastline are sweet-looking craft—well cared for by the factories that own them, ready at a moment's notice to steam to a remote cove or the wind-swept backside of Seal Island to pick up her load of 50 to 80 hogsheads of fish. This old measure of volume is still used to indicate a boat's capacity—a hogshead is 17 bushels—and when the two holds are filled to the hatch coamings, the fisherman knows exactly how many fish he has sold.

Pauline, considered by many to be the prettiest and best kept of all the carriers, was modeled in 1948 by Roy Wallace of Thomaston, and built by the Newbert and Wallace yard. This firm had turned out a long string of large wooden hulls for the fishing fleet—draggers, scallopers, and a number of sardine carriers—and were well known for quality work and fair prices. Double-sawn oak frames and two inch yellow pine planking ensures a stiff, durable hull that can stand the hard driving and heavy loads of sardine carrying. *Pauline* is powered by a Cummins 324 horsepower diesel driving a large, slow-turning propeller for maximum efficiency. These long, narrow hulls drive easily with relatively little power and seem to go nearly as well loaded as light.

Several years ago, looking for a place to go ashore, we tied *Northern Crown*, our thirty-five foot cutter, alongside *Pauline* in Carver's Harbor, Vinalhaven. Her captain, Henry Dodge, and mate, "Swede" Carlson, made us welcome and invited us aboard to look her over. After admiring her functional simplicity and immaculate appearance, I went back aboard *Northern Crown* hoping that the vicissitudes of the sardine industry would not affect her future. Unfortunately, it was not to be: *Pauline* is now for sale, a victim of changing times and the mysteries of the herring schools.

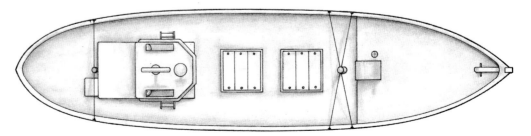

Designer: Roy Wallace   Builder: Newbert and Wallace, 1948

CIRRUS

is red and beautiful. Above her "special red" topsides, a wide band of varnished teak top strake and rail stretch from bow to stern, with a gold-leaf cove stripe separating the two and accentuating the sheer. Her sheer line is classic and without blemish. When the wind is right, she heels to the gold stripe, which dances just above the rushing leeside wave, her sheer exactly conforming to the water bent by her passage. Her white sails above are reflected in the waters below. Under sail, she is a picture; once seen, she is not soon forgotten. There is nothing quite like her.

You cannot separate the man from the yacht. Alan Bemis, her owner for fifty years, is as much a part of her as her keel. He loved her, cared for her, enjoyed her, and perfected her over those fifty years, even down to her "special red" topside paint. When he decided a few years ago that the time had come to part with her, all those who knew the man and the boat felt the wrench of separation.

Cirrus was built by Herreshoff in 1930 (as *Kelpie*), one of fourteen boats known as the Fishers Island 31-foot class. The 31s are a development of the earlier Newport 29 class, already noted as speedy boats. The new boats had longer overhangs, straighter sheer, and generally more room below. *Cirrus* was one of several which was built to extra high specifications, with teak sheerstrakes, rails, cabin sides, and deck trim. As with all Herreshoff-built boats, her scantlings are on the light side for a boat of her size, but fifty-eight years of trouble-free service argue for their correctness. Design, materials, and craftsmanship of the order put into *Cirrus* are simply not available today.

LOA:	44′ 0″
LWL:	31′ 0″
Beam:	10′ 9″
Draft:	6′ 2″

The original rig of these boats was a low aspect ratio sloop, with a single set of spreaders and small jib. Alan, always one to sail fast, raised the headstay higher on the mast, added a set of diamond shrouds to support it, purchased a genoa jib, and began winning races. In 1954, Alan decided to make her a yawl, and my first paid naval architectural commission was to draw the new sail plan. A mizzenmast was added, the long main boom shortened, and she continued to win races, as well as being a much easier boat for short-handed sailing. Alan sailed her alone much of the time, when there were no family or friends about, and one of the great summer sights on Eggemoggin Reach used to be Alan and *Cirrus* setting off from High Head into the face of a rising afternoon southerly.

In 1980, Alan hosted a memorable fiftieth birthday party for *Cirrus*. Several other Fisher Island 31s arrived under sail, plus many other boats and friends. The guest of honor floated at her dock, fully dressed, to receive the admiration of the assembled crowd. Launches carried the crews ashore from the anchored yachts to the party in the stone house just above the dock. Looking out the picture window onto the dock scene below, it was easy to time-warp back several decades, when all boats were wooden, and I was just a boy sailing a Herreshoff 12½, wonderstruck at the big red sloop rushing by to windward in a smother of foam.

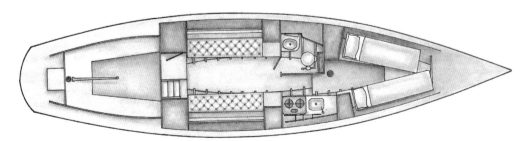

Designer: N. G. Herreshoff   Builder: Herreshoff Mfg. Co., 1930

TWILITE

is a re-creation of the past—the past of almost exactly a century ago. She is a faithful reproduction of J. Henry Rushton's *Vesper* canoe, the original being built in 1886 for a young canoeist named Robert W. Gibson. With the original *Vesper*, Gibson won the International Challenge Cup that summer in a race between the Americans and the British—a sort of America's Cup for canoes. In 1975, using the same techniques and materials Rushton used, Everett Smith built a replica of *Vesper*'s hull for Bob LaVertue of Springfield, Massachusetts. Bob built the rig, most of the hardware, and named the boat *Twilite*. A decked canoe with oval cockpit, batwing ketch rig, brass plate rudder, and a folding metal centerboard, she offers all the visual delights of design and craftsmanship of those earlier canoes, while providing insight to the design as conceived by our grandfathers.

LOA: 15' 6"
LWL: 15' 4"
Beam: 2' 6"
Draft: 0' 5"

Perhaps a little history of organized canoeing in America is in order. Oddly enough, canoeing as a sport was a British idea that crossed the Atlantic around 1860.

John MacGregor, a Scot and a religious zealot, was an advocate and practitioner of "muscular Christianity," a concept originating in Europe on the premise that athletic activity and energetic sportsmanship would lead one to the upright life and therefore closer to God. MacGregor chose to fulfill his quota of athletic achievements by cruising most of the waterways of the Continent in

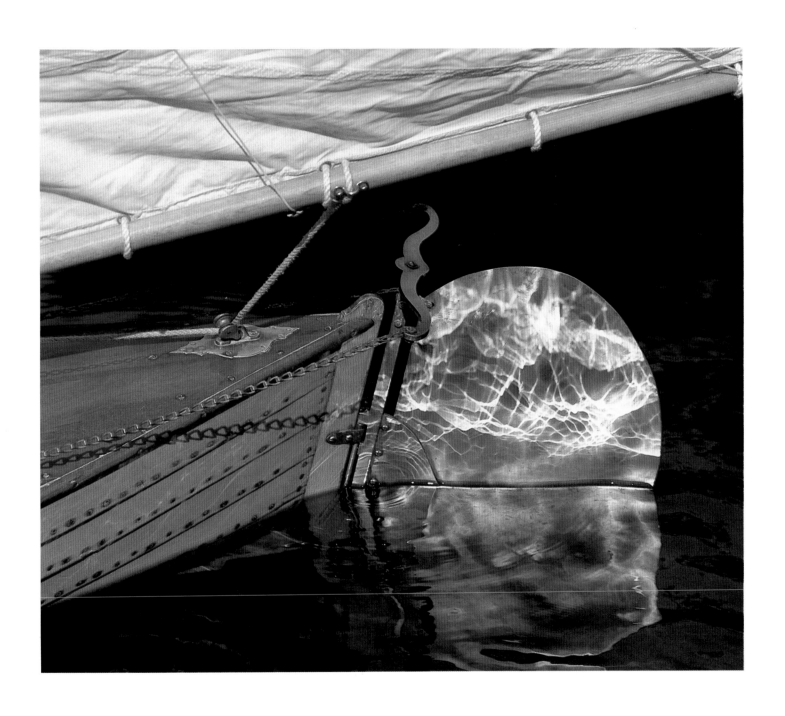

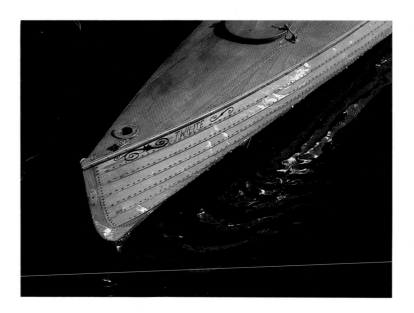

canoes of his own design, all named *Rob Roy*. Several books by MacGregor about his canoe voyaging found wide audiences in both Europe and America, making him more successful as an advocate for canoeing than for philosophy. However achieved, uprightness must always be a virtue greatly desired by anyone messing about in tiny canoes with a beam of less than eighteen inches!

In any case, his American readers absorbed the gospel of MacGregor and the joys of canoeing. Soon clubs devoted to the sport were formed in various areas of the eastern United States. In 1880, the American Canoe Association was founded at Lake George, New York. From a charter group of twenty-three in 1880, membership rose to sixteen hundred twenty-five in 1889, and canoeing as a sport had become established.

Beneficiary of all this interest in canoes was J. Henry Rushton, a boatbuilder from the small Adirondack town of Canton, New York. Rushton was a fine craftsman with a knack for publicity, and soon canoeists were coming to his shop to talk over new designs of light, strong, cedar canoes for the growing market. Rushton was a man unafraid to try something new—and soon a series of small, very light canoes, culminating in a nine foot model named *Sairy Gamp*, weighing only ten and a half pounds, spread his fame throughout the American canoe world.

The all-wood cedar canoe was of course dependent on fine craftsmanship for its watertightness, rather than an outer skin of painted canvas. Built with light cedar lapstrake planking over very small, closely-spaced elm frames, all held together with clenched copper tacks and small brass screws, the wooden canoe was (and is) a true art-form of fine boatbuilding. Its light weight was greatly prized for ease of portaging and transporting. Rushton ran a sizeable shop from 1873 until the time of his death in 1906. Towards the end of the century, a severe depression (plus the sudden popularity of the bicycle) caused a serious decline in canoe building; its appeal as a sport dropped dramatically.

After a long hiatus, canoeing and kayaking have returned to great popularity with our athletic and recreation-minded enthusiasts—both male and female. *Twilite* stands out in this modern crowd of small watercraft, a throwback to an earlier time, a different drummer. Built from trees rather than petroleum or metal, by the meticulous craftsmanship of one man, rather than the anonymous labor of mass production, she reminds us of how far we have come—or gone.

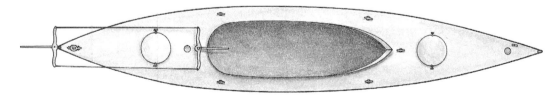

Designer: J. Henry Rushton   Builder: Everett Smith, 1975

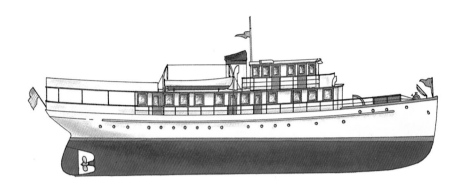

CANIM

is a "Yacht" with a capital Y, all ninety-six feet of her. Designed by Ted Geary, she was built by Lake Union Dry Dock Co. in 1930 for Col. C. B. Blethen of Seattle, Washington. Blethen was the flamboyant owner of the *Times*, Seattle's largest daily newspaper, and a man not averse to making a splash. *Canim*, which in Haida Indian means "big chief's canoe," was Blethen's idea of how to make a splash in Seattle in 1930. That must have been a banner year for yacht building, as I know of several other fine craft first launched that year, including two in this book, *Cirrus* and the Herreshoff 12½ *Shadow*.

LOA: 95' 9"
LWL: 89' 6"
Beam: 18' 4"
Draft: 7' 6"

The big chief didn't keep her long, however—the Depression was in full swing, and it was hard times for yachting. After a checkered career all over the West Coast, she wound up back in Seattle with a caring owner who refitted *Canim* to her original elegance and condition. Looking at these pictures, you can see the quality of her original build, and the amount of care, maintenance, and restoration that has gone into her recently. She probably seems even more stunning now than when she was new, if only because we are no longer used to this degree of elegance in yachts.

Canim has all the earmarks of a 1930 power yacht—plumb stem, vertical boxy deck structures, and a canoe or "steamboat" stern. Elliptical on deck with a heavily raked profile, this stern reverses at the waterline into a bustle over the propeller and rudder. I believe the thinking on this shape was to have the hull swell out over the propeller to prevent air from being sucked down and causing cavitation. It also provides extra buoyancy aft, and helps prevent squatting. In any case, this kind of stern is seldom seen today, perhaps because of the difficulty of its construction.

Her hull and panelled deckhouse are painted gloss white, contrasting with the varnished teak rails, window frames, and doors, red boot top, and red painted accents around the rim of the stern and her upper handrails. All this is punctuated by twenty round brass portlights per side, each carefully polished!

Below, *Canim* again says "Yacht" with a capital Y. Panelled bulkheads in natural wood, beautiful carved moldings, carpeted soles, and a marble-faced fireplace. Everywhere there is a feeling of understated elegance, quiet comfort, and good taste. At night, the interior is illuminated by polished brass light fixtures with shell-pattern glass shades.

The elliptical sweep of bulwarks aft encloses the lounge area at the stern. Here the teak deck and panelled bulwarks in natural finish contrast with the white-painted overhead. Handsome rattan chairs and couches with white pillows invite the owner's party to relax around the glass-topped coffee table. Want to sunbathe?—up one flight on the aft end of the boat deck, protected by canvas weathercloths to keep out the wind and envious stares.

Several years ago *Canim* attended the Classic Boat Festival in Victoria, B. C., where these pictures were taken. This event attracted one hundred forty of the finest yachts in the Pacific Northwest, which were judged in a number of different categories, even including Best Costumed Crew. *Canim* was awarded prizes for Best Powerboat Overall, and Best Powerboat Restoration.

Canim is perfectly suited to her cruising area. Imagine a leisurely voyage from Seattle up the inside passage behind Vancouver Island to Desolation Sound, and return. A lovely older yacht lending a sense of timelessness to some of the world's finest maritime scenery.

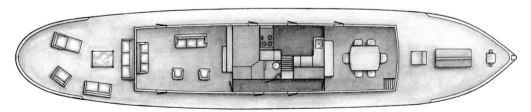

Designer: Ted Geary   Builder: Lake Union Dry Dock Co., 1930

CHRISTMAS

LOA: 44′ 9″
LWL: 34′ 0″
Beam: 12′ 0″
Draft: 7′ 6″

was built in 1931, well over a half-century ago, yet her appearance is that of a sensible wooden cruising boat of the 1950s. Her good looks, enhanced by a lovely sheer and a handsome canoe-stern, lead to speculation as to the identity of her designer. Further investigation reveals that she was drawn by W. Starling Burgess, and built by Eastern Shipbuilding Corp. of Shelburne, Nova Scotia.

Burgess was a designer of tremendous talent, and wide-ranging abilities. He was a pioneer in early aircraft design, as well as having a full career in naval architecture. Volatile, charismatic, and with the unpredictability often associated with genius, he is best known as a designer of racing craft: the America's Cup defenders *Enterprise* and *Ranger*; the fast Gloucester fishing schooners *Mayflower*, *Puritan* and *Columbia*; and *Niña*, an ocean-racing staysail schooner that Burgess himself considered to be his favorite design. But his long string of purely cruising designs, such as *Christmas*, have the same beautiful proportions and careful engineering as his better-known racing creations.

Her lines show a hull of very heavy displacement, with high, slack bilges, steep deadrise, and little reverse curve to the garboards. This hull form depends on a lot of ballast for stability. To move all this displacement and ballast through the water, a generous cutter rig with long main boom, and large fore-triangle provides the energy to drive *Christmas*.

Study the spacious deck layout of *Christmas*, with her wide side decks, high bulwarks, narrow cabin trunk, comfortable cockpit, self-tending staysail sheet, and sheets and running backstays led aft to the cockpit for convenience. All of this speaks of crew comfort on deck and easy handling of the rig.

Phillip LaFrance had been the professional captain of *Christmas* before becoming her owner in 1979. Well aware of her needs, he started a major rebuilding and refitting program. This included a number of new frames, some replanking, replacement of the after backbone, and a complete refastening by replacing the original planking screws with copper rivets. Following the hull rebuilding, a new interior was installed. After two years, *Christmas* was sound and seaworthy again.

Mr. LaFrance uses *Christmas* for occasional charters, enters her in classic yacht races, and sails her for his own pleasure. With good care, and some luck, the omens for her next fifty years are good.

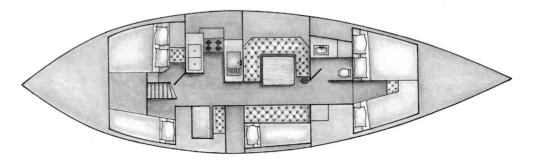

Designer: W. Starling Burgess   Builder: Eastern Shipbuilding Corp. Shelburn, N. S., 1931